Today's Choral Classics

Beautiful music for mixed-voice choirs from inspiring composers.

NOVELLO

Published by
Novello Publishing Limited
14-15 Berners Street,
London W1T 3LJ, UK.

Exclusive Distributors:
Music Sales Limited
Distribution Centre, Newmarket Road,
Bury St Edmunds, Suffolk IP33 3YB, UK.

Music Sales Corporation
257 Park Avenue South,
New York, NY 10010, USA.

Music Sales Pty Limited
20 Resolution Drive, Caringbah,
NSW 2229, Australia.

Order No. NOV292941
ISBN 978-1-78038-586-0

Music processed by Paul Ewers Music Design.

Printed in the EU.

www.chesternovello.com

Contents

A BLUE TRUE DREAM OF SKY 1
Judith Weir

A BOY AND A GIRL 9
Eric Whitacre

A GOOD-NIGHT 15
Richard Rodney Bennett

ALLELUIA JUBILATE 21
James Whitbourn

AVE VERUM 35
Timothy Noon

CRUCEM TUAM ADORAMUS, DOMINE 41
Paweł Łukaszewski

KYRIE 47
Richard Blackford

MOTHER OF GOD, HERE I STAND 49
John Tavener

NUNC AUTEM MANET 53
John Duggan

O VERA DIGNA HOSTIA 59
Tarik O'Regan

QUANTA QUALIA.. 70
Patrick Hawes

SET ME AS A SEAL 76
Nico Muhly

THE LORD'S PRAYER 87
John Tavener

THIS MARRIAGE.. 91
Eric Whitacre

UBI CARITAS... 97
Richard Allain

UBI CARITAS... 110
Paul Mealor

WHEREVER YOU ARE.. 116
Paul Mealor

in honour of Philip Brunelle

a blue true dream of sky

e. e. cummings

Judith Weir

* the solo altos should, if possible, be positioned
apart from the main body of the chorus;
for instance, in an alcove or gallery.

4

Commissioned by the 2002 California All-State Choir

A Boy and a Girl

for Dr Ron Kean

Octavio Paz

Eric Whitacre

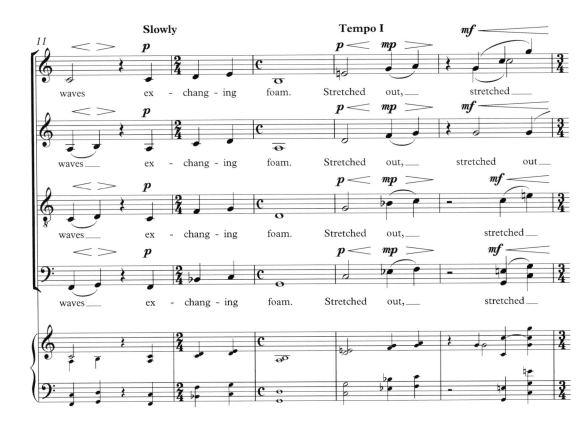

out ___ on the beach ___ a boy and a girl.

___ on the beach ___ a boy and a girl.

out ___ on the beach ___ a boy and a girl.

out ___ on the beach ___ a boy and a girl.

Sa - vouring their ___ limes, ___ giv - ing their kiss - es ___ like

Sa - vouring limes, ___ giv - ing their kiss - es ___

Sa - vouring limes, ___ giv - ing their kiss - es ___

Sa - vouring limes, ___ giv - ing their kiss - es ___

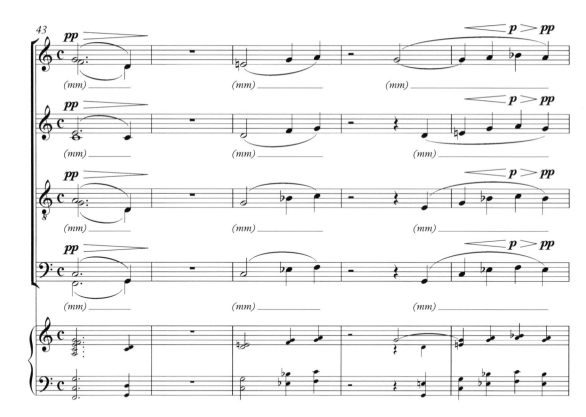

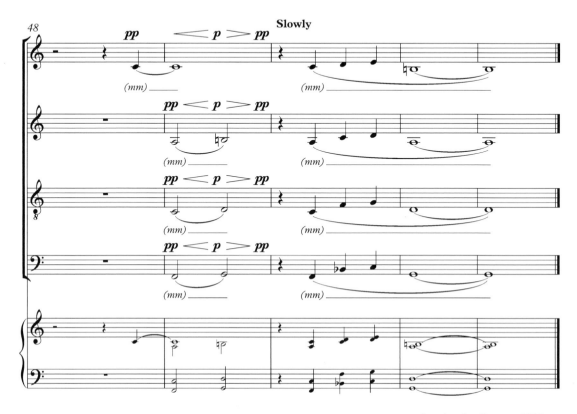

Los Angeles, January 2002

for Paul, in memory of Linda

A Good-Night

Francis Quarles
(1592–1644)

Richard Rodney Bennett
(1999)

20

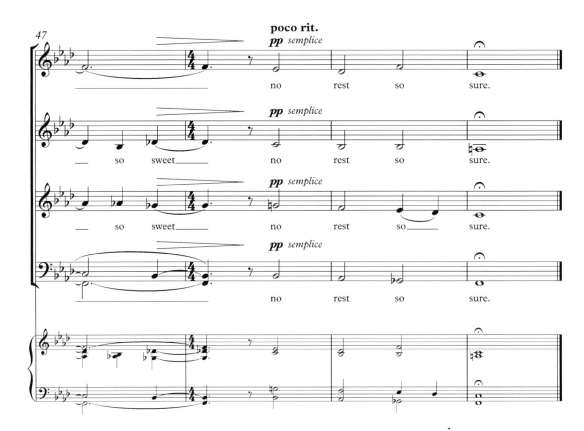

Commissioned for the Choir Schools' Association conference 2008, originally for upper voices

Alleluia jubilate

From Psalm 66 (65): 1-2
(Introit of the Third Sunday of Easter)

James Whitbourn

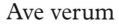

For Canterbury Cathedral Choir

Ave verum

Fourteenth-century hymn

Timothy Noon

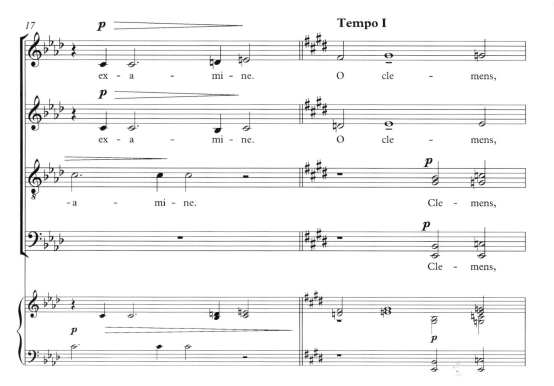

Tempo I

ex - a - mi - ne. O cle - mens,

ex - a - mi - ne. O cle - mens,

-a - mi - ne. Cle - mens,

Cle - mens,

O pi - e, O dul - cis, O Je -

O pi - e, O dul - cis, O Je -

O pi - e, O dul - cis, O Je -

O pi - e, O dul - cis, O Je -

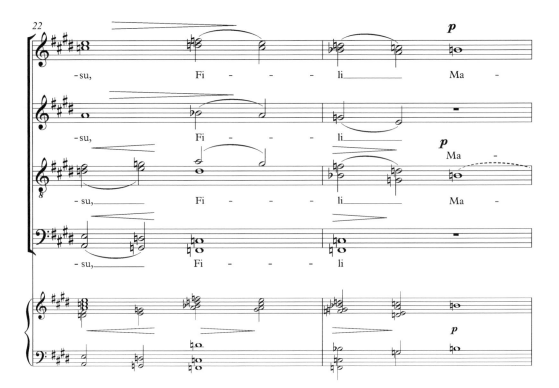

rallentando al fine

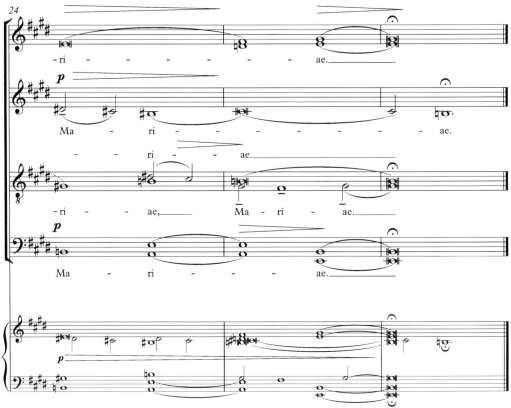

Provence, 16 August 2000

Crucem tuam adoramus, Domine

from Two Lenten Motets

Paweł Łukaszewski, 1995

Kyrie

Richard Blackford
(2006)

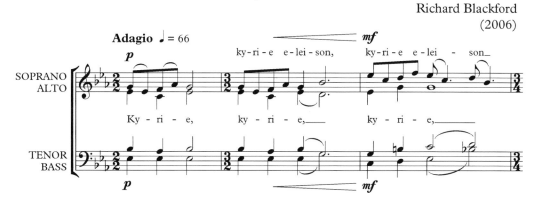

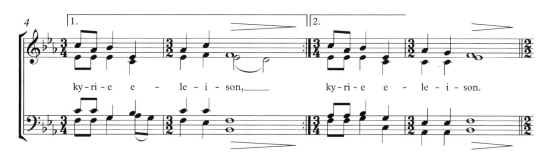

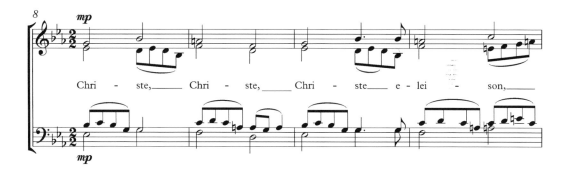

48

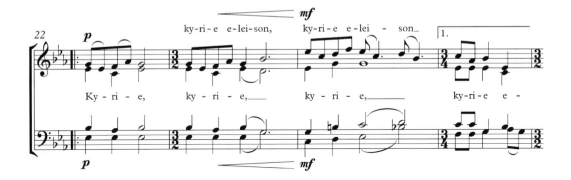

Mother of God, here I stand

from The Veil of the Temple

John Tavener

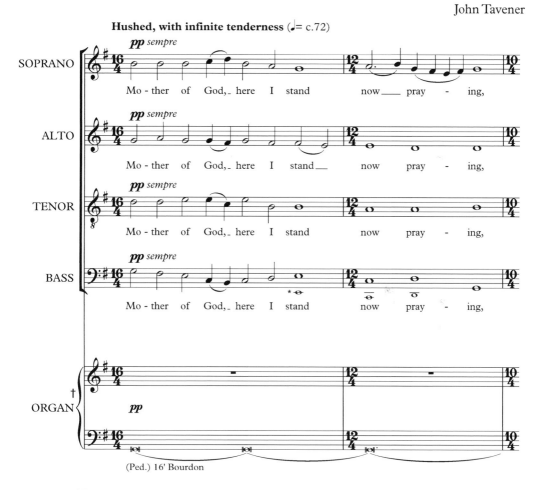

* Bass 2 is optional throughout
† Play only if necessary to keep the choir up to pitch

50

for Paul & Angharad

Nunc autem manet

John Duggan

Commissioned by *The Vaulkhard Choral Trust* for
The Choir Schools' Association

O vera digna hostia

from
SEQUENCE FOR ST. WULFSTAN

First performed in Winchester Cathedral at Evensong on 6th May,
2003 by Winchester Cathedral Choir directed by Andrew Lumsden

Latin text sourced from MS 391, p.
247: Cambridge, Corpus Christi Col-
lege (the Portiforium of St Wulfstan)

Translation: J. M. Neale (1818 - 1886)

Tarik O'Regan

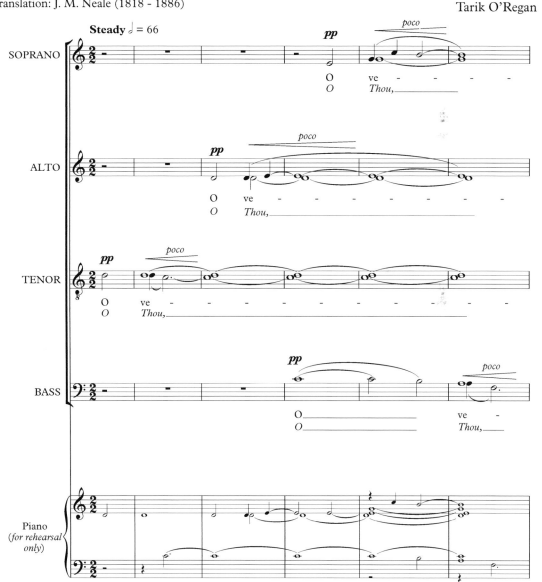

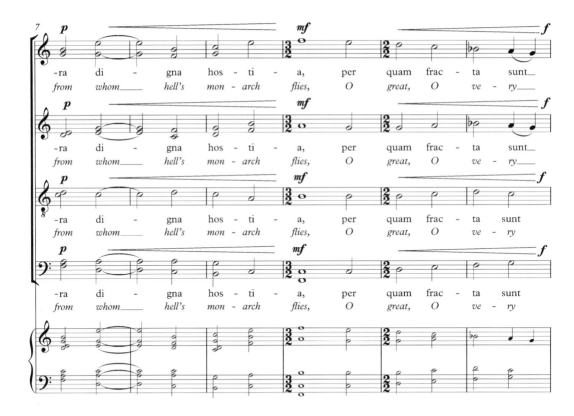

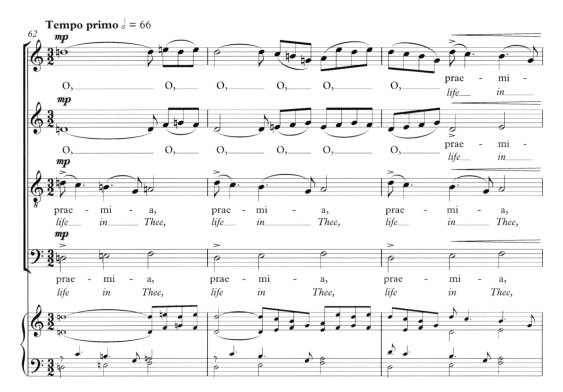

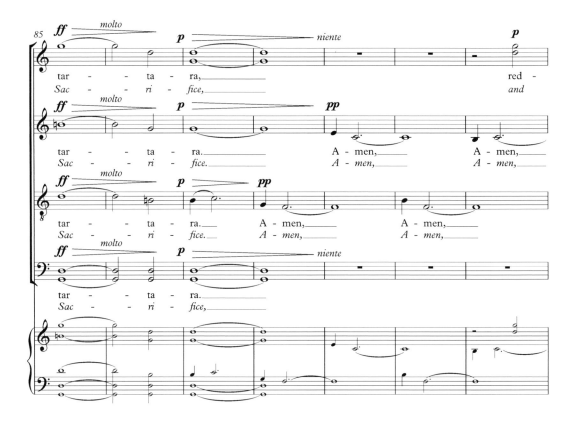

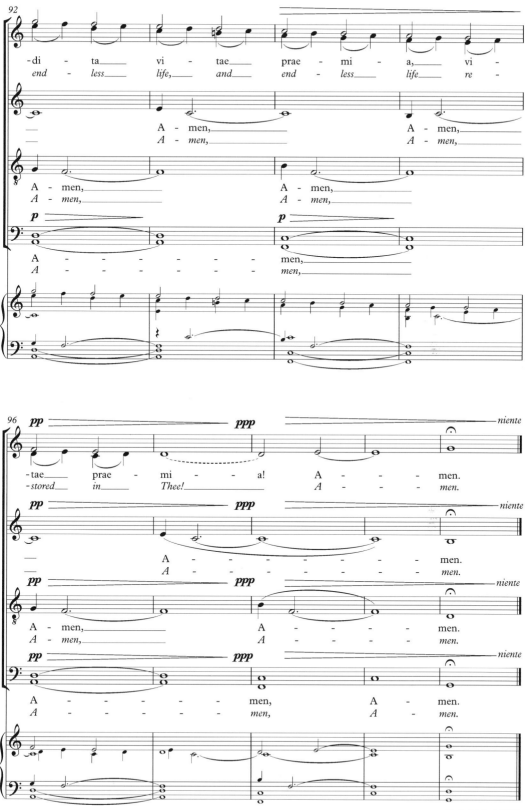

Oxford, March 2003

Quanta qualia

Andrew Hawes

Patrick Hawes

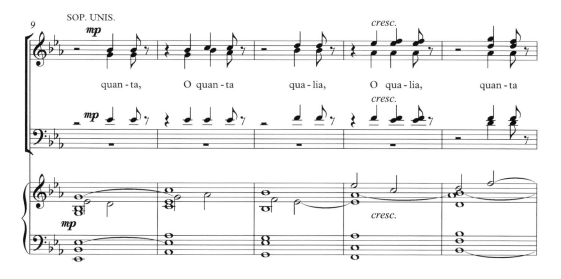

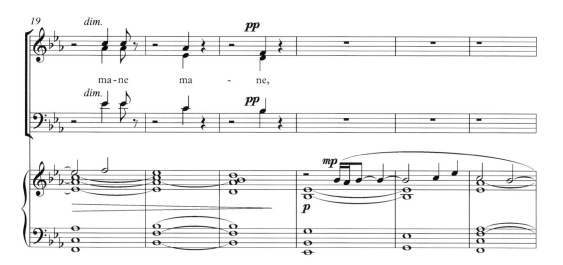

qua - lia con - ven - tus, gau - dia, con - ven - tus

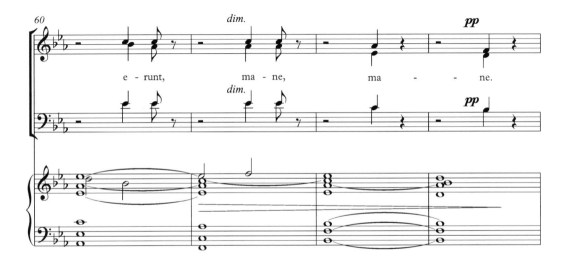

e - runt, ma - ne, ma - ne.

SOPRANO
SOLO

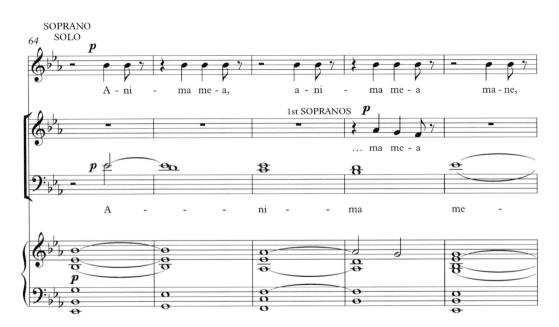

A - ni - ma me - a, a - ni - ma me - a ma - ne,

1st SOPRANOS

... ma me - a

A - - - ni - - ma me -

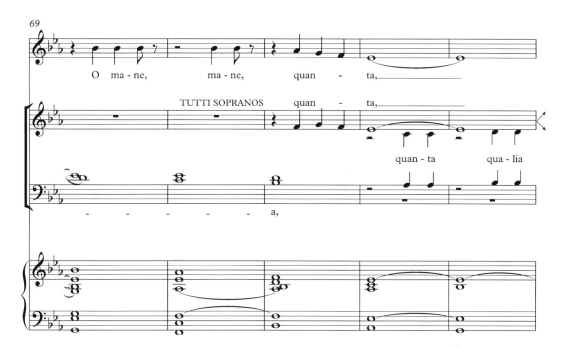

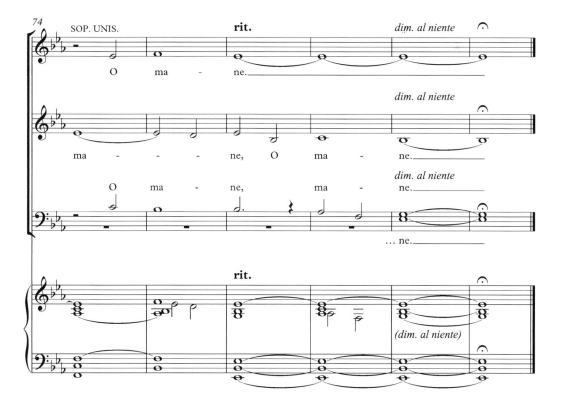

for Judy Clurman

Set me as a seal

Nico Muhly

84

86

for the birth of Charlotte

The Lord's Prayer

John Tavener
(1999)

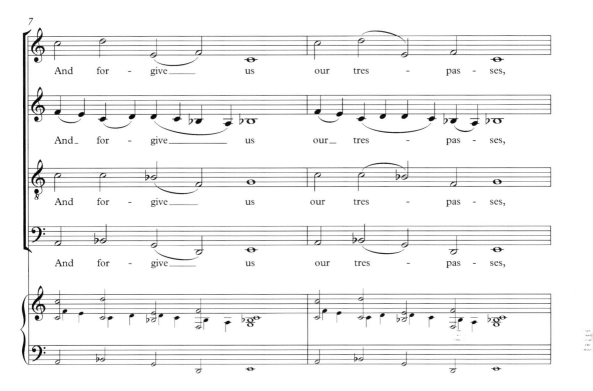

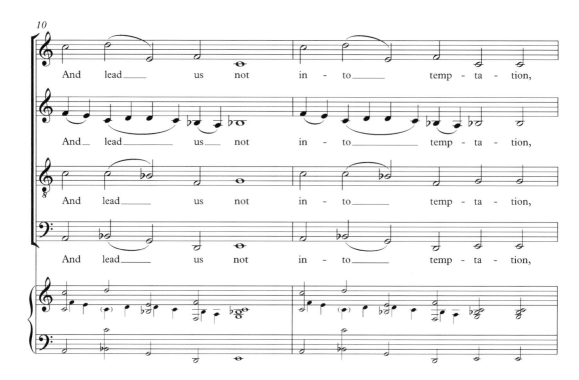

Naldretts, 4th June, 1999

Commissioned by Azusa Pacific University for
The APU Chamber Singers, Michelle Jensen, conductor

This Marriage

for Hila on our seventh anniversary

Jalal Ad-din Rumi

Eric Whitacre

Senza misura, freely and tenderly

SOPRANO: May these vows and this mar - riage be bless - ed.

ALTO: May these vows and this mar - riage be bless - ed.

TENOR: May these vows and this mar - riage be bless - ed.

BASS: May these vows and this mar - riage be bless - ed.

Piano *(for rehearsal only)*

SOPRANO: May it be sweet milk, like wine and hal - vah.

ALTO: May it be sweet milk, like wine and hal - vah.

TENOR: May it be sweet milk, like wine and hal - vah.

BASS: May it be sweet milk, like wine and hal - vah.

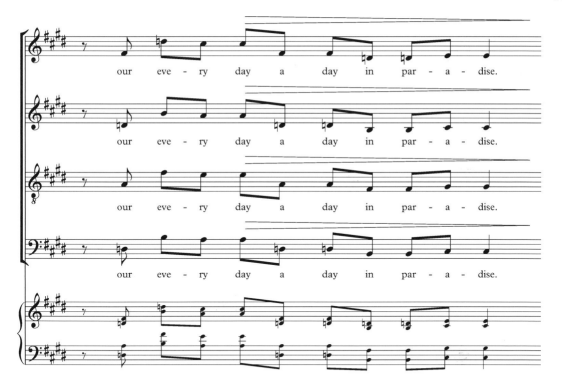

our eve - ry day a day in par - a - dise.

our eve - ry day a day in par - a - dise.

our eve - ry day a day in par - a - dise.

our eve - ry day a day in par - a - dise.

May this mar - riage be a sign of com - pas - sion,

May this mar - riage be a sign of com - pas - sion,

May this mar - riage be a sign of com - pas - sion,

May this mar - riage be a sign of com - pas - sion,

a seal of hap-pi-ness, here _____ and here-af-ter.

May this mar-riage have a fair _____ face and a good _____ name,

an o - men as wel - comes the moon in a clear blue sky.

an o - men as wel - comes the moon in a clear blue sky.

an o - men as wel - comes the moon in a clear blue sky.

an o - men as wel - comes the moon in a clear blue sky.

I am out of words to de - scribe how spi - rit min - gles in this

I am out of words to de - scribe how spi - rit min - gles in this

I am out of words to de - scribe how spi - rit min - gles in this

I am out of words to de - scribe how spi - rit min - gles in this

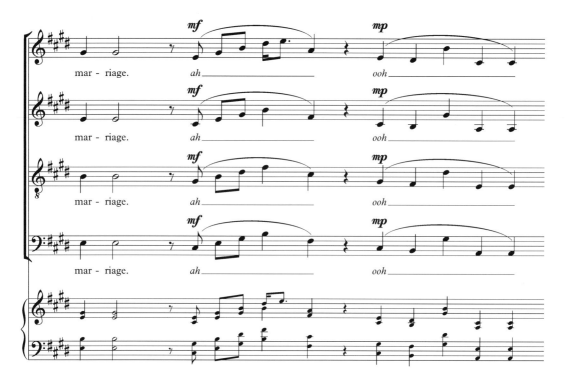

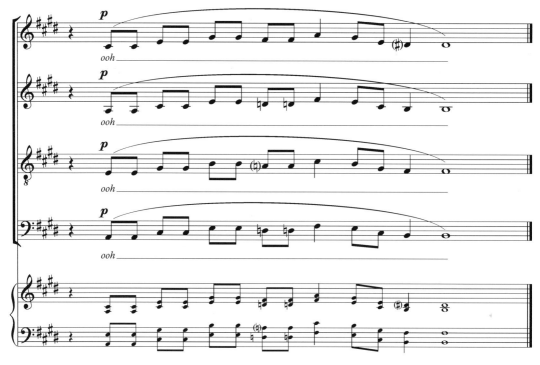

Los Angeles, October 2004

Ubi Caritas

Richard Allain

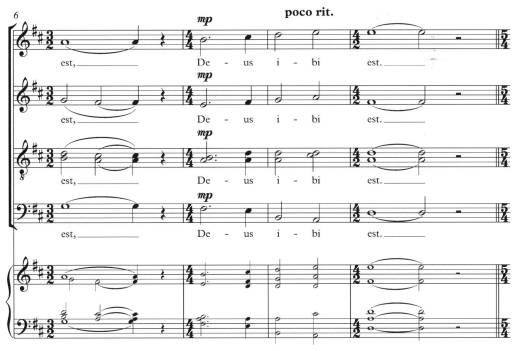

This anthem may be performed tutti throughout, or with two choirs as indicated.

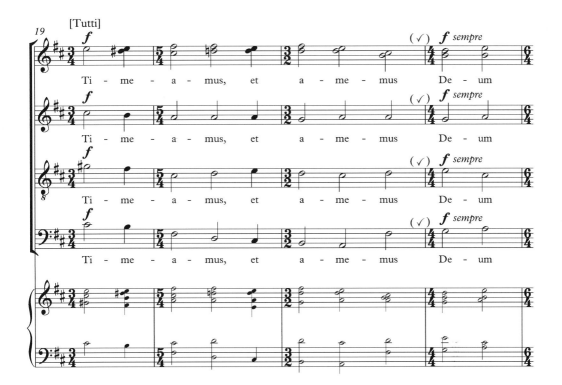

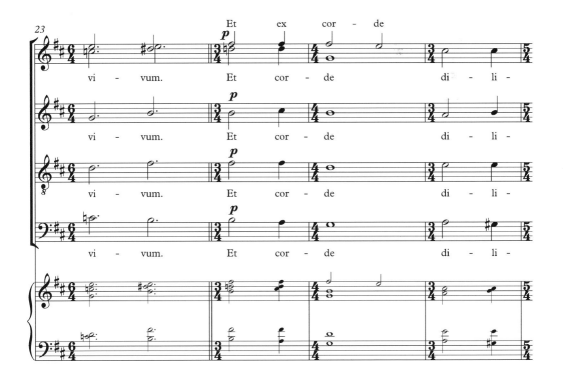

Tempo I

[Choir II]

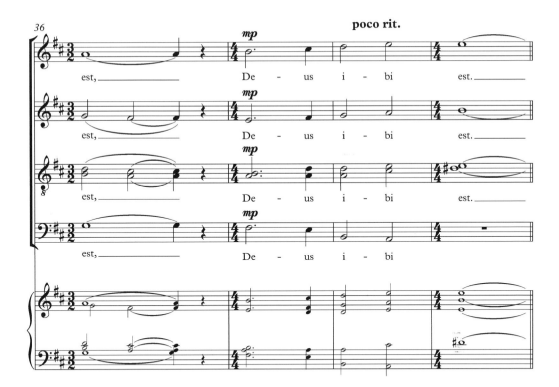

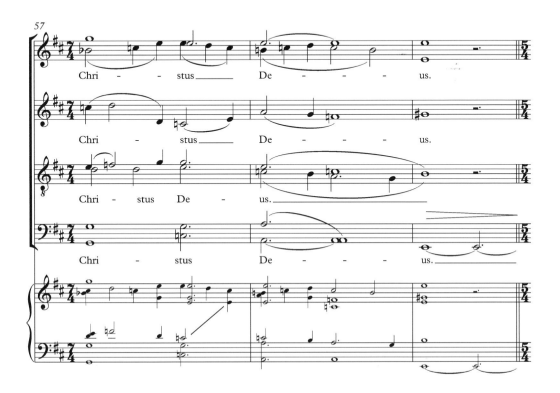

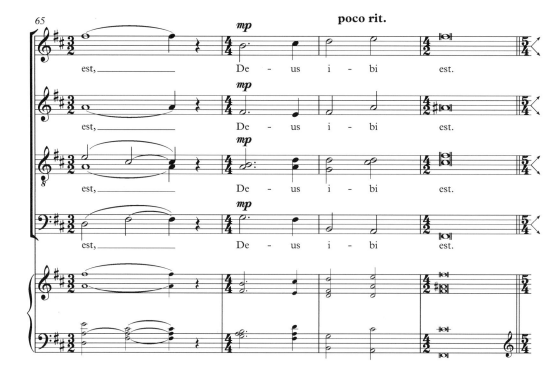

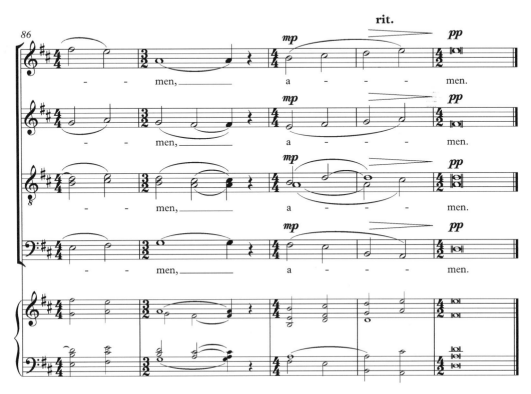

Mill Hill 17.10.04

Ubi caritas

Paul Mealor

112

molto rit.

vi - vum.___ Et ex___ cor - de di - li - ga - mus___ nos sin - ce - ro.

vi - vum.___ Et ex cor - de di - li - ga - mus___ nos sin - ce - ro.

vi - vum.___ Et ex___ cor - de di - li - ga - mus___ nos sin - ce - ro.

vi - vum.___ Et ex___ cor - de di - li - ga - mus___ nos sin - ce - ro.

* Bracketed notes are optional divisi.

B

poco rit.

mf *f*

U - bi ca - ri - tas et a - mor,___ De - us___ i -

mf *f*

U - bi ca - ri - tas et a - mor,___ De - us i -

mf *f*

U - bi ca - ri - tas et a - mor,___ De - us i -

mf *f*

U - bi ca - ri - tas et a - mor,___ De - us i -

Solo
(This may be sung 'off stage' if desired)

Dedicated to Gareth Malone and The Military Wives

Wherever you are

The Military Wives' Prayer

Paul Mealor

love will keep you safe;____ My____ heart will build a bridge of light a-

love will keep you safe;____ My____ heart will build a bridge of light a-

-cross both time and space.____

-cross both time and space.____

(Tutti) *pp*

I____

(Tutti) *pp*

I____

Wher - ev - er you are,____ our____ hearts still beat as one,____ I____

Wher - ev - er you are,____ our____ hearts still beat as one,____ I____